BUSES OF MOTOR COACH INDUSTRIES

1932 THROUGH 2000
PHOTO ARCHIVE

William A. Luke and
Brian Grams

Iconografix
Photo Archive Series

Iconografix
PO Box 446
Hudson, Wisconsin 54016 USA

Library of Congress Card Number: 00-135948

ISBN 1-58388-039-9

01 02 03 04 05 06 07 5 4 3 2 1

Printed in the United States of America

Cover and book design by Shawn Glidden

Copy editing by Dylan Frautschi

Cover Photo: Northwestern Stage Lines of Spokane, Washington, has been a Motor Coach Industries customer for a number of years. In 1999, the company purchased two of the Renaissance® Coaches. Another was added in 2000. In the summer months these luxury buses are assigned to Tauck Tours.

Book Proposals

Iconografix is a publishing company specializing in books for transportation enthusiasts. We publish in a number of different areas, including Automobiles, Auto Racing, Buses, Construction Equipment, Emergency Equipment, Farming Equipment, Railroads & Trucks. The Iconografix imprint is constantly growing and expanding into new subject areas.

Authors, editors, and knowledgeable enthusiasts in the field of transportation history are invited to contact the Editorial Department at Iconografix, Inc., PO Box 446, Hudson, WI 54016.

ACKNOWLEDGMENTS

Photographs in this book are from the bus history libraries of the authors, Brian Grams and William A. Luke, unless noted as photo credits from other individuals and organizations.

The following persons and organizations were very helpful in providing support, information and pictures that have made this book possible.

Steve Bacovsky, President National Motor Coach, Calgary, Alberta

Athena Campos, Motor Coach Industries, Schaumburg, Illinois

Steve Casarin, Motor Coach Industries, Winnipeg, Manitoba

Donald Coffin, Greyhound Lines Historian, Hawley Pennsylvania

David Dyck, Director of Maintenance, Greyhound Canada, Calgary, Alberta

Andrew Gold, Computing Support Analyst, Calgary Transit, Calgary, Alberta

Walter Grams, Retired Greyhound Driver, Calgary, Alberta

Cheryl Heilman, National Marketing Manager, Greyhound Canada, Calgary, Alberta

Paul Leger, President, Bus History Association, Halifax, Nova Scotia

Patricia Plodzeen, Patricia Plodzeen Public Relations, Chicago, Illinois

Chris Redbourn, Motor Coach Industries, Winnipeg, Manitoba

Table of Contents

FOREWORD

Motor Coach Industries is proud of the role it has played in the history of motor coach transportation and is grateful to Bill Luke for his chronology of MCI motor coach models.

With this book, which captures nearly every MCI model ever made, Bill demonstrates his passion for the industry, and his friendship with the people of MCI. As founder of what has become one of the most notable magazines of its kind, Bill has dedicated himself to promoting this industry by writing about it. His words are worth reading and these pictures telling.

We also extend our appreciation to Brian Grams, a collector of bus and coach memorabilia, for contributing many of the photos from his personal collection.

Most of all, we owe our deepest thanks to the coach owners and operators whose names grace these pages. We feel privileged to be the maker of the equipment that serves them and their businesses every day.

Sincerely,

Roberto Cordaro
Chief Executive Officer
Motor Coach Industries

INTRODUCTION

Motor Coach Industries had its beginnings in Winnipeg, Manitoba, on April 9, 1932. The original name of the company was Fort Garry Motor Body and Paint Works.

The company was founded by Harry Zoltok, who went into partnership with Fred Sicinski. They established a 5,000 square foot plant on Fort Street in Winnipeg.

In 1933 the first bus was built. It was a stretched design using a large Packard sedan. Then, in 1937, the firm designed and constructed its own chassis and completed a bus for Grey Goose Bus Lines of Winnipeg.

Central Canadian Greyhound Lines took an interest in the Fort Garry company and had several of their Model Y Yellow Coach buses rebuilt by Fort Garry. Greyhound officials were impressed with the quality of the rebuilt buses.

Two Model 37-UM buses, with Hall-Scott under-floor gasoline engines, steel construction, and seating for 37 passengers, were built for Central Canadian Greyhound in 1938. The initial order was followed by a further order for four more buses.

The next model produced by Fort Garry was the Model 33-UE. Central Canadian Greyhound ordered 10 in 1940. This coach had aluminum siding, which was being used in bus construction at that time.

In 1940, Central Canadian Greyhound was purchased by the Greyhound Corporation and the new company was named Western Canadian Greyhound Lines. It was this company that ordered twelve coaches in 1940 to be delivered in 1941. This coach was the famous Alaska Highway bus. Officially they were the Model 37-UE, but they became known as the "600s" as they were fleet numbers 601 to 612 for Greyhound. They were leased to the Northwest Service Command but driven by Canadian Greyhound employees.

On January 7, 1941, the name of the Fort Garry Motor Body and Paint Works was changed to Motor Coach Industries. At about the same time a new 20,000 square foot plant at Erin and St. Matthews in Winnipeg was acquired.

During World War II, Motor Coach Industries stopped building buses and was fully committed to the war effort building trailers, army truck bodies, and a variety of other products for the armed forces. In the immediate post war years bus manufacturing resumed but some diversification continued.

Western Canadian Greyhound continued to have a close relationship with Motor Coach Industries. On July 14, 1948, Western Canadian Greyhound bought shares in Motor Coach Industries. As the Greyhound Corporation in the United States owned Western Canadian Greyhound Lines, Greyhound in the United States became owner of an interest in Motor Coach Industries.

The Couriers 100, 85, and 95 were some of the post war models of Motor Coach Industries. These models, at first, had International Red Diamond gasoline engines. A Courier 85 was the first MCI to have a diesel engine. That was in 1951 and the engine was a Cummins diesel. The Model 95 began using General Motors diesel engines and was the first MCI model to have air suspension.

During the 1960s, there was significant growth at Motor Coach Industries. The MC-1, introduced in 1959, was followed by the MC-2, MC-3, MC-4, and finally the MC-5. All were 35-foot buses with diesel engines and air suspension and had many refinements over previous models.

Through Greyhound Lines of Canada, Greyhound Lines in the United States became full owner of Motor Coach Industries in 1958. Also, in the latter part of the 1950s, a 62,000 square foot expansion of the original plant was completed.

With an eye to selling coaches in the United States, Motor Coach Industries Incorporated (MCI) was established on April 2, 1962 in Pembina, North Dakota. A factory was opened there for final assembly of bus shells built in Winnipeg. That set the stage for Motor Coach Industries' MC-5 buses to be sold to Greyhound in the United States. The first "shell" was shipped to Pembina on September 13, 1963 and the first completed coach came off the Pembina plant line later that same month. The MC-5 was also being sold to other bus companies not only in Canada but also in the United States at that time.

In 1968, a 134,000 square foot building was erected on a 24-acre site in the Winnipeg suburb of Fort Garry. By 1968 the 40-foot MC-7 was developed and placed in production. The Model MC-6 was also being developed at the same time. The MC-6 was a 40-foot bus but 102 inches wide with a V-12 diesel engine. It was built especially for Greyhound.

The growth of Motor Coach Industries was supported by an expanded sales organization plus the development of a strong service organization. From a production of 39 buses in 1960, 500 buses were being built each year by the end of the 1960s.

The MC-8 was introduced in 1973 and it was followed by the MC-9 in 1978. The MC-9 became the North American intercity bus industry's all-time best selling bus.

MCI's new appearance buses were introduced in 1984 as the 96A3 and 96A2. Upgrades of the series followed including increasing the width to 102 inches. These were 40-foot models, and, in 1992, a 45-foot bus was introduced. It is known as the Model 102DL3.

For a period from 1987 through 1993, Motor Coach Industries was also involved in producing transit buses, the RTS bus in Roswell, New Mexico, and the Classic bus in St-Eustache, Quebec.

During the 1990s, Motor Coach Industries experienced two ownership changes. In 1994, Corsorcio G. Grupo Dina of Mexico merged with Motor Coach Industries. In 1999, the investment company of Joseph Littejohn and Levy became the majority owner of the company.

Motor Coach Industries had a small beginning but has emerged to become a world-class manufacturer of buses.

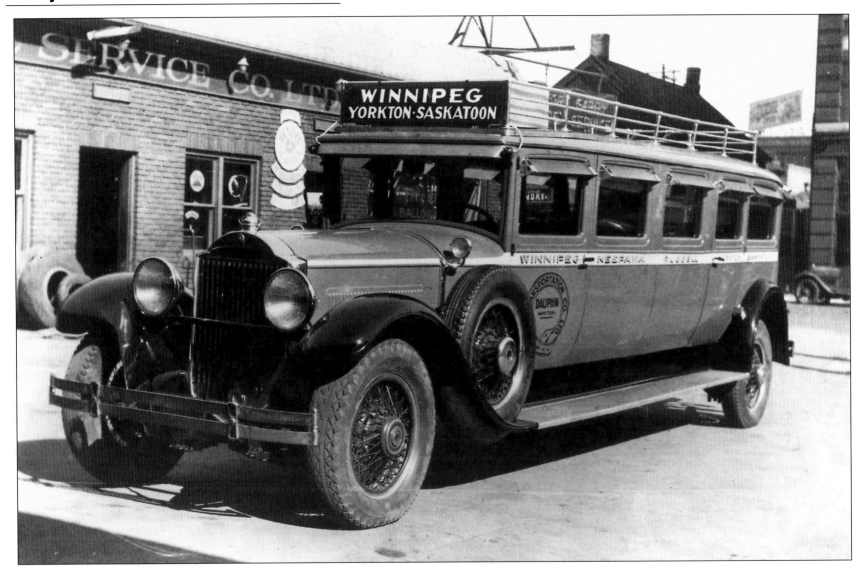

The first bus built by the Fort Garry Motor Body and Paint Works (predecessor of Motor Coach Industries) was this Packard in 1933. The vehicle was originally a large Packard sedan and Fort Garry stretched it by adding a new center section.

Gray Goose Stage was one of the early bus companies buying buses built by Fort Garry Motor Body and Paint Works. The body was mounted on a Canadian Maple Leaf truck chassis (GM). Gray Goose Stage operated this bus in the late 1930s on routes in Saskatchewan.

This bus was built by the Fort Garry Motor Body and Paint Works in Winnipeg in 1938 for Central Canadian Greyhound Lines. It had a 6-cylinder under-floor Hall-Scott gasoline engine. It is pictured at the Winnipeg, Manitoba, Bus Terminal.

Pictured at the Edmonton, Alberta, bus terminal is this Fort Garry Motor Body and Paint Works Model 33-UE, a 33-passenger bus built for Central Canadian Greyhound Lines in 1940. It had a Hall-Scott under-floor gasoline engine. Buses of Central Canadian Greyhound like this one were also called "150s" because the fleet numbers were 150-159.

In 1942, twelve buses built the year before by Motor Coach Industries for Western Canadian Greyhound Lines were assigned to Alaska Highway Service. The service was operated under the Northwest Service Command. These buses, like the one pictured here, had Hall-Scott under-floor engines.

The original Motor Coach Industries plant was located in Winnipeg, Manitoba, at the corner of Erin and St. Matthews. It was acquired in 1941 and had 20,000 square feet of space. Motor Coach Industries moved to a 134,000 square foot building in the 1960s.

In 1942, Motor Coach Industries designed and built this trolley bus, Model TRY for the Winnipeg (Manitoba) Electric Company. It remained in service until May 1960 and was the only trolley bus built by MCI. A scarcity of materials and excessively high import duties on traction motors at that time resulted in the trolley bus not becoming a regular production model.

Western Canadian Greyhound Lines fleet number 501 was the prototype Courier 100. It is shown here at the MCI plant in Winnipeg in 1946. This was the first rear engined MCI, had 33 seats, and used the International RD 450 gasoline engine.

Eagle Bus Lines operated suburban bus service northeast of Winnipeg, Manitoba, after World War II. The Motor Coach Industries Courier 100, pictured here, joined the Eagle fleet in 1946.

This 1947 Motor Coach Industries Courier 100 was operated by Beaver Bus Lines Ltd. of Winnipeg, Manitoba. It was powered by an International Red Diamond gasoline engine. Beaver Bus Lines operated bus service between Winnipeg and Selkirk, Manitoba. The line and this coach were acquired from the Winnipeg Electric Co., which originated this bus route.

Pictured here are seven Model 200 Motor Coach Industries buses. They were part of an order for 12 Model 200 MCIs added to the Eastern Canadian Greyhound fleet in May 1948. The Courier 200, which had one extra window per side, 37 seats, and the Continental gasoline engine, were otherwise similar to the Courier 100.

There were 95 Motor Coach Industries Courier 200 buses built. Western Canadian Greyhound Lines received 65, including this one, which was built in 1948. The Eastern Canadian Greyhound fleet had an additional 28 Courier 200 buses.

This is a 1949 Courier 100B. The Greyhound dog emblem on the side looks just like the one that is used today. Greyhound used the Courier 100s mainly on the Canadian Rockies route between Calgary and Vancouver.

The Motor Coach Industries Courier 200B, shown here, was delivered to Eastern Canadian Greyhound Lines in Windsor, Ontario, in 1949. It had a rear-mounted Continental six-cylinder gasoline engine.

In 1950, MCI introduced the Courier 50 to replace the Courier 100. Available as an option on this coach were sight-seeing windows on the roof. These were the first MCI "Skyviews." This is one of two Courier 50 "Skyviews" that were new to Brewster Transport of Banff, Alberta, in 1950. It is posed at the end of the main street in Banff with Cascade Mountain in the background. Photo Credit: *Whyte Museum of the Canadian Rockies*

Two Courier 50 "Skyviews" work their way through the switchbacks of the road coming from Takakkaw Falls in Yoho National Park. Yoho is in British Columbia just west of Banff National Park. Rocky Mountain Motor Tours of Banff, Alberta, operated the "Skyviews" in this picture.

This Motor Coach Industries Courier 85 was a 37-passenger bus operated by Thiessen Transportation, Ltd. of Steinbach, Manitoba. Thiessen Transportation was founded in 1946. This Courier 85 joined the Thiessen fleet in 1951. The Courier 85 had rear-mounted International Red Diamond 450 gasoline engines.

This is a 1952 Motor Coach Industries Courier 85 from Canadian National Transportation. This coach worked a Boston schedule but did not go all the way through. Passengers could ride this coach from Glace Bay, Nova Scotia, to St. Stephen, New Brunswick, where they would change to a Maine Central coach to go to Boston. Photo Credit: *Paul Leger*

Built in 1952, this Model 90 Courier "Skyview" is parked at the Crowfoot Glacier view-point on the Banff Jasper Highway in the Canadian Rockies. Photo Credit: *Whyte Museum of the Canadian Rockies*

The first diesel engines used in production by MCI were four-cylinder GM Diesels in the Courier 95 in 1953. This is a photo of the third such coach built and was part of a group of five for New England Greyhound Lines. The order marked the first sale of an MCI coach to a U.S. operator.

The Courier 95 was the first MCI model sold to the Saskatchewan Transportation Company. This bus was built in 1954 and was powered by a four-cylinder GM Diesel engine. Typical Courier 95s had 37 seats.

The Courier 95 being built at the Erin and St. Matthews plant in Winnipeg. The photo was taken in 1955 and this coach was earmarked for Western Canadian Greyhound Lines when the company bought a total of 57 Courier 95s.

A companion model to the Courier 95 was the Courier 96, which had 41 seats and was 35 feet long. This is a 1958 MCI Courier 96 and was operated by Newmarket Coach Lines, Ltd., of Newmarket, Ontario.

This is a Courier 96 built in 1959, one of the last 96s built. All 96s had the four-cylinder GM Diesel engine and most were air ride but a few were built with spring suspension.

The photo is of an MC-1 built in 1959. The MC-1 was the first of the Challenger series. It still used the four-cylinder GM Diesel engine and was 35 feet long with 41 seats.

This is a Motor Coach Industries MC-2 built in 1960. Restrooms and air-conditioning were available on the MC-2, although this coach had neither. There were some styling changes from the MC-1. The big news was the use of the V-6 GM diesel engines with a five-speed standard transmission. Sorensen Bus Lines, Ltd., of Red Deer, Alberta, operated this bus.

This MC-2 was one of five delivered to Gray Coach of Toronto in May of 1961. A feature of the MC-2 was the widely spaced taillights and the fluting on the engine doors, which was different than on the MC-1.

Grey Goose of Winnipeg bought this MC-2 in 1961. It had air-conditioning and a restroom. The photo was taken in Winnipeg beside the football stadium used by a Canadian football team, the Winnipeg Blue Bombers.

This is an MC-3 built in 1963 for Sunburst Lines in Edmonton, Alberta. It still used the V-6 GM diesel with a five-speed standard transmission. It sold new for $42,774.00. Photo Credit: *Provincial Archives of Alberta*

Trans Canada Highway Tours was operated by Greyhound Lines of Canada. The tours ran between Calgary and Vancouver. This Motor Coach Industries Model MC-4 was one of the 16 acquired by Greyhound in 1963. All of these 16 MC-4s had restrooms and air-conditioning.

There were 50 MC-4s built. All were built in 1963 and 15 of them went to Gray Coach Lines of Toronto. The MC-4 was the first MCI to use the V-8 GM Diesel and a four-speed standard transmission.

This is a 1964 MCC-5. The second "C" in the model designation indicates that the bus was completely built in Canada. Until the introduction of the MC-5 series in 1963, Motor Coach Industries had built less than one thousand coaches. The MC-5 was the first MCI model to be exported to the United States in any quantity and more than 2,500 of the MC-5/5A/5B/5C series were built. This bus was operated by SMT (Eastern) Limited of St. John, New Brunswick. Photo Credit: *Paul Leger*

When Motor Coach Industries began selling buses in the United States, this MC-5A demonstrator was shown to many bus companies throughout the country. The MC-5A is pictured here on display at the American Bus Association annual meeting in Phoenix, Arizona, in 1965.

This very pretty 1966 MCI MC-5A belonged to Greyhound Lines of Canada. The special paint job was for a VIP service between Lethbridge, Alberta, and Edmonton, Alberta.

This Motor Coach Industries Model MC-5A was one of 675 MC-5A buses delivered to Central Greyhound Lines in 1966. The Greyhound companies in the United States and Canada bought 1600 of the MC-5/5A/5B series buses.

Another MC-5A, this one owned by Canadian Coachways of Edmonton, Alberta. This one is a 1967 model and later became part of the Greyhound fleet in 1969 when Greyhound purchased Coachways.

An MC-5A for MacKenzie Bus Line of Nova Scotia, Canada. This one was used to transport the Don Messer Jubilee Show on a Canadian tour.

California-Nevada Golden Tours operated tour and charter service in the Reno/Lake Tahoe area. The company was one of the first independents to operate Motor Coach Industries buses in the United States. Pictured here is a model MC-5A.

This Motor Coach Industries Model MC-5B of Winn Bus Line in Richmond, Virginia, was painted red, white, and blue in a special design to celebrate the U.S. Bicentennial. The bus received a first place award by *Bus Ride* magazine for the best intercity Bicentennial painted design.

From 1975 to 1976, Yellowstone Park Company purchased 25 Motor Coach Industries MC-5B buses for sight-seeing in Yellowstone National Park. Shown here is one of the buses at Mammoth Hot Springs. Nine of these MC-5B buses continue their sight-seeing service after 25 years.

Greyhound Canada bought ten of the Motor Coach Industries Model MC-5Bs, four in 1975 and six more in 1976. So far, this is the last 35-foot coach purchased by the Greyhound companies. This is an MCI factory photo and the fleet number has not been applied.

An MC-5B "Skyview," which was new to Brewster Gray Line of Banff. This photo was taken in Jasper, Alberta, deep in the Canadian Rockies. The Brewster glasstop 5Bs had a V-6 Detroit Diesel with an Allison automatic transmission.

A Brewster Transport MC-5C "Skyview." This one was built in 1978 and had the V-8 Detroit Diesel engine with a four-speed standard transmission.

In the late 1970s, Greyhound Lines entered into a joint venture in Saudi Arabia to operate bus service for the Arabia American Oil Co. compound at Al Kohbar, Saudi Arabia. There were 198 Motor Coach Industries Model MC-5C buses in the service. All were built with a special double roof to protect against the hot Arabian sun and 149 buses had two doors as shown in this photo. There were 30 1981 Motor Coach Industries Model MC-9 buses operated as well.

A Brewster Gray Line MC-5C "Skyview" lines up for a parade in Banff, Alberta. The parade celebrated 100 years of business in Banff for this company.

In far-off Guam, the Gray Line company operates this 1980 Motor Coach Industries Model MC-5C. Gray Line Guam acquired it as a used bus in December 1988. Originally the bus was in service with Continental Air Transport in Chicago, Illinois.

This is the first of two MC-6 prototype buses built by Motor Coach Industries in 1967. The MC-6 was 102 inches wide, 40 feet long, and was built with the V-12 Detroit Diesel engine with a four-speed standard transmission. This photo was taken in Calgary as the MC-6X toured North America prior to going into production in 1969. The "X" in the MC-6X designation indicated that the bus was an experimental model.

Greyhound Canada received 15 of the 100 Motor Coach Industries Model MC-6 buses built. Greyhound Canada used the MC-6 buses on long distance routes especially between Toronto and Vancouver. In 1969 Greyhound held a contest to name the new coach and "Supercruiser" was chosen.

Greyhound Canada had 15 MC-6s. They were all built in 1969. This picture of fleet number 346 was taken in 1971 at the start of a VIP service from Calgary, Alberta, to Edmonton, Alberta.

The first production MCI 40-foot coach was actually the MC-7. There was a production run in 1968 prior to the building of the MC-6. This photo was taken outside the Jubilee Auditorium in Calgary and shows the doors over the tag axle wheels. These doors were used on early MC-7s, as well as the early MC-6s.

Peoria-Rockford Bus Company of Rockford, Illinois, entered into a niche market in 1962 operating non-stop "Silver Arrow" bus service between Rockford and Chicago's O'Hare Airport. Two Motor Coach Industries MC-7 buses were acquired for the service in 1968. This MC-7 was added the following year.

In late 1969, some changes were made to the MC-7 and these buses came to be known as the "Super Sevens." This "Super Seven" was new to Grey Goose in Winnipeg. Note the new style baggage doors and different front cap. This is a 1970 MC-7 with 47 seats, restroom, and a V-8 Detroit Diesel engine with a four-speed standard transmission.

Greyhound bought 400 Motor Coach Industries MC-7s in 1971. This bus was one of 178 that went to Western Greyhound Lines. Greyhound in the United States added 1,400 MC-7 buses to its fleet between 1968 and 1973. The later Greyhound MC-7s were called "Super 7 Scenicruisers."

Ontario Northland Transportation, a division of Ontario Northland Railway, which is based in North Bay, Ontario, purchased two Motor Coach Industries Model MC-7 buses in 1972. They had two and one seating and the schedule they operated was advertised as "Sleeper Service."

Motor Coach Industries shipped ten Model MC-7 kits to Australia for final assembly in 1972. These buses went into service for Ansett Pioneer Express, a leading long distance bus company in Australia at that time. Later Motor Coach Industries buses for Australia were completely built in Winnipeg and Pembina, North Dakota.

Greyhound Lines of Canada first added Motor Coach Industries Model MC-7 buses to its fleet in 1968 when the model was first introduced. The MC-7 bus is 40-feet long and has a Detroit Diesel 8V-71 diesel engine. This is a 1972 MC-7 at the Castle Mountain viewpoint just west of Banff, Alberta.

Model MC-8

Airport Service of Anaheim, California, took delivery of 10 Motor Coach Industries Model MC-8 buses in 1974. This picture was taken in front of the Theme Building Complex at the Los Angeles Airport.

This Greyhound Lines Motor Coach Industries Model MC-8 was one of the 13 gas turbine powered buses that Greyhound operated experimentally. It had a Detroit Diesel Allison GT404-3 engine and was part of a U.S. Department of Energy program. Although there were numerous advantages with turbine engines, there were more disadvantages and the program was discontinued.

Frank Martz Coach Line of Wilkes-Barre, Pennsylvania, a member of the National Trailways Bus System, bought this Motor Coach Industries MC-8 bus and seven others in 1974. Martz Trailways operates from several Northern Pennsylvania communities to New York City, as well as several other routes.

New Mexico Transportation Company of Roswell, New Mexico, was the owner of the first bus built at the Transportation Manufacturing Corporation plant in Roswell. Later, New Mexico Transportation was acquired by Texas, New Mexico & Oklahoma Coaches, now a fully owned Greyhound company.

This is the Transportation Manufacturing Corporation plant in Roswell, New Mexico. TMC started production in 1975 and most of their coaches went to Greyhound U.S. These are MC-8 Americruisers under construction.

The first Goodyear blimp bus was a 1930 Flxible. In 1976, after a long history of purchasing Flxible products, Goodyear needed another bus and Flxible was no longer building highway coaches. Goodyear bought their first MCI MC-8 that year and added 2 more in 1978. The 1978 coaches were among the last of the MC-8s built and do not have the slanted center roof pillar.

This is a 1976 MC-8 for Yellow Coach Lines of Edmonton, Alberta. It has a V-8 Detroit Diesel engine and a four-speed automatic transmission. The Yellow Coach name was later abandoned and all the remaining coaches were moved to the Grey Goose Bus Lines fleet. This photo was taken in Calgary just above the Stampede Grounds.

This picturesque winter scene shows a Greyhound Motor Coach Industries MC-8 bus traveling over Stevens Pass between Seattle and Spokane, Washington.

Americruiser number 2000 rolls out of the TMC plant in Roswell, New Mexico, on September 11, 1978. Greyhound U.S. used the name Americruiser for their MC-8s while Greyhound Canada continued with Scenicruiser.

In 1978, Motor Coach Industries delivered 50 Model MC-8 buses to the Republic of China through its Taiwan Highway Bureau. These buses operated on a modern North-South freeway between Taipei, the capital of Taiwan and Kaohsiung, a major port city. Buses operated on a 15-20 minute headway during the day on the 373-km (232-mi) route.

A Brewster Gray Line MC-8 "Skyview" poses just west of Banff, Alberta. Brewster continues to be the main tour operator in Banff National Park, which is Canada's largest National Park and the second largest National Park in North America after Yellowstone.

This is the prototype MC-9. It is the first of what would become the most popular highway coach ever built. When MC-9 production was stopped in 1994 there had been some 9,500 MC-9s built.

This Motor Coach Industries MC-9 and eleven others were delivered to the South African bus manufacturer BUSAF in 1979. The twelve MCIs were then operated by the South African Railways bus service. The picture shows one of the MC-9s in sight-seeing service in Cape Town in 1983. Photo Credit: *Wilhelm Pflug*

This Motor Coach Industries MC-9 bus was purchased by Indian Trails of Owosso, Michigan, in 1979 with 14 others. Indian Trails had a total of 52 MC-9 buses. Indian Trails' main route is between Flint, Michigan, and Chicago, Illinois. Each Indian Trails bus is named for an important Indian chief.

A Motor Coach Industries MC-9 of Greyhound Lines of Canada poses in the Canadian Rockies at a viewpoint west of Calgary, Alberta. Greyhound Canada called their MC-9s the "Scenicruiser 2" rather than the "Americruiser 2" used by Greyhound U.S.

Orange Belt Stages of Visalia, California, added two MCI MC-9 buses to its fleet in 1980. They were painted a bright orange with black trim. Orange Belt bus number 178 is shown at a colorful balloon rally. Orange Belt Stages traces its roots back to 1916.

In 1981, GO Transit added Motor Coach Industries MC-9 buses to its 185-bus fleet. GO Transit is a large Government of Ontario bus service operating in the Toronto area. It began in 1970.

In 1986, Organizacion Nacional de Autobuses (ONDA S.A.) of Montevideo, Uruguay, operated Motor Coach Industries buses including this Model MC-9. ONDA operated a number of intercity routes within Uruguay as well as several international routes. One of the important ONDA routes linked Montevideo with Buenos Aires, Argentina.

These three Motor Coach Industries Model MC-9s were referred to as Careliners by America West Airlines. The buses operated from various Phoenix, Arizona, suburban communities to the Phoenix Sky Harbor Airport. They were allowed to drive to the airside of the terminal giving passengers direct access to the aircraft. The MC-9s were leased from Arizona Southern Bus Lines of Phoenix. Note the beacon light on top of the buses for airside travel.

This is one of two MC-9s built in 1982 as demos prior to the production run of coaches to be used by New Jersey Transit. The production "Jersey Cruisers" had a new front cap with a large destination sign centered above the windshields. This is known as the Jersey cap.

On the 50th anniversary of the Alaska Highway in 1992, Greyhound Lines of Canada operated regular service over the highway from Dawson Creek, British Columbia, to Whitehorse, Yukon. Pictured here is Greyhound Lines of Canada fleet number 699, a 1982 Motor Coach Industries MC-9 at Milepost Zero on the Alaska Highway.

Greyhound Canada has been a good customer for the MCI MC-9, buying more than 250 of them. Most have more than two million life miles now and over half have been sold to other operators.

Ansett Pioneer Express of Australia purchased 15 Motor Coach Industries Model MC-9 buses in 1984. The buses were built in Winnipeg and Pembina, North Dakota, with the entrance door on the left side and the driver position on the right for Australian rule of the road requirements. In 1976, Ansett Pioneer purchased 10 Motor Coach Industries MC-8 buses.

This is an MC-9 built by Transportation Manufacturing Corporation for Suburban Transit of New Brunswick, New Jersey. The bus has a two-leaf entrance door, which was specified by many operations using the bus in commuter and suburban transit service. Suburban Transit operates this type of service and also contracts with the State of New Jersey for several routes.

Bonanza Bus Lines of Providence, Rhode Island, was one of the first bus companies to operate the MCI MC-9 model. Between 1979 and 1984 there were 38 MCI MC-9 buses acquired by Bonanza. This was the only two-axle MCI MC-9 in the Bonanza fleet. It was built by Transportation Manufacturing Corporation. Some states allowed two-axle buses and Bonanza was able to use this bus on some of its routes.

This 1989 MCI MC-9 is the only factory-built MC-9 combo coach. (A combo coach is one that has a combination of space for packages in the rear and passengers in the front.) All other Greyhound combo coaches were converted from regular passenger models.

This is a 1990 Motor Coach Industries MC-9 "Special." It is owned by Greyhound Canada and generally runs north out of Edmonton, Alberta. Note the use of the "storm front" on the coach. Even the MCI MC-9 can use some help when running down the highway at seventy miles per hour and the temperature outside is minus forty degrees. This photo was taken in Calgary where the coach had just gone through a major inspection. It will now work its way back to its Edmonton home base.

The Motor Coach Industries MC-9 was in production from 1978 to 1994. More MC-9s were built than any other highway coach ever. The later MC-9s have come to be called the MC-9 Specials. The last MC-9 was built in 1994 as a prison inmate transportation vehicle. This MC-9 is the last of four purchased by Grey Goose Bus Lines of Winnipeg in 1990.

In 1992, Greyhound Lines in the United States began a bus replacement program. It was decided to rebuild the fleet with a bus similar to the successful and proven Motor Coach Industries MC-9 bus. The result was the MC-12 model, which incorporated some modification from the MC-9. Greyhound received more than 1300 of these buses between 1992 and 1998. This MC-12 is pictured at St. Regis, Montana, where Greyhound schedules a meal break for its passengers.

One of the last Greyhound Lines (GLI) MC-12 coaches delivered, fleet number 3171, leaves the Toronto Bus Terminal bound for Chicago. Greyhound's MC-12 buses built after late 1996 were equipped with Detroit Diesel Series 50 4-cylinder, 4-cycle engines. Photo Credit: *Andrew Gold*

For a short period between 1987 and 1992 Motor Coach Industries was also involved in the manufacturing of transit buses. The production facilities were acquired from General Motors of Canada when they left the bus industry. The Classic model transit bus that was inherited from GM was built in the ex-GM factory in Saint-Eustache, Quebec. This example is one of 34 buses built for Winnipeg Transit in 1988.

In 1985, Greyhound Canada bought 25 of the Model 96A3, all with the Detroit Diesel 6V-92TA and a five-speed standard transmission.

This is a 1985 Motor Coach Industries Model 96A3. It was built as a 47-passenger coach, but has been converted to a 30-passenger combination (combo) coach. This allows a very large freight area at the back. The restroom is now in the middle of the bus.

This 1985 Model 96A2 bus joined the Gray Line Guam fleet in November 1989. It was acquired from Hausman Bus Sales. It originally operated in the New York City area. Note the bus has two axles and a transit style door.

Gray Line of Alaska purchased 36 Model 96A3 buses built by Transportation Manufacturing Corporation of Roswell, New Mexico, in 1986. There were twenty buses ordered without lavatories that were used for short sight-seeing services. This bus was assigned to Gray Line of Alaska's Juneau operation. It is pictured here with the famous Mendenhall Glacier in the background.

Greyhound Canada started buying the 102A3 in 1986. Originally equipped with the Detroit Diesel 6V-92TA, two of them have been retrofitted with a Caterpillar 3176B diesel engine and are used to haul Greyhound Parcel Express trailers.

GO Transit continues to operate the MCI 102A2 in commuter service in southern Ontario. Note the two-piece transit-type door, an option chosen by many MCI customers. Photo Credit: *Andrew Gold*

This 102A3 is a factory-built 35-passenger combination (combo) coach. The combo coaches have a shortened passenger compartment to allow room for a rear cargo area. There were four MCI Model 102A3 combo coaches built, all for Grey Goose Bus Lines. They still serve northern routes in Manitoba, many of which involve travel on gravel roads.

This is one of the fleet of 162 wheelchair accessible Motor Coach Industries Model 102A3 coaches delivered to the Dallas (Texas) Area Rapid Transit in 1991.

This is a 1992 Motor Coach Industries Model 102B3. It is basically a 102A3 with painted sides. This bus was acquired by Greyhound Canada when Greyhound bought Gray Coach of Toronto, Ontario, from Stage Coach Holdings. Photo Credit: *Andrew Gold*

Prior to going to Antelope Valley in California, this Motor Coach Industries Model 102C3 bus was the MCI sales demo coach number 941.

This is the line up for the service lanes in Calgary, Alberta. Calgary is the largest shop for Greyhound Canada. Fleet number 850 is a 1989, 47-passenger MCI Model 102C3.

It says MCI on the front but it is a 1990 TMC 102C3. This coach does tour and charter work for Laidlaw Canadian Rockies.

Beaver Bus Lines is shown earlier in this book with a Courier 100. The company has since grown into one of the largest charter operators in Manitoba and one of their coaches is this MCI 102C3.

In 1994, four-cycle six-cylinder in-line diesel engines became standard equipment to meet tightening emission regulations. To accommodate the increased length of engines such as the Detroit Diesel Series 60, the 102D3 with a shortened wheelbase replaced the 102B3 and 102C3 series. A revised lower body structure and baggage compartment arrangement was introduced. The larger single radiator, optionally available since 1992, became standard equipment.

In 1992, 45-foot intercity buses were made legal in the United States. At that time Motor Coach Industries introduced the Model 102DL3 bus. The longer buses had increased seating capacity, normally for 55 passengers. Pictured here is one of the first MCI 45-foot buses.

The summer of 1995 finds this MCI 102DL3, operating for Tauck Tours, parked outside of the Chateau Lake Louise. It is owned by Accent Lines of Calgary and has a Caterpillar 3176B diesel engine with a seven-speed standard transmission.

Royal Dutch Airlines (KLM) wanted special transportation to and from Montreal's Mirabel Airport and Quebec City for its overseas passengers and offered bus-connecting service. This Motor Coach Industries 102DL3 had special graphics for KLM. It was operated by Autobus Viens, Inc. of Saint-Jean-sur-Richelieu, Quebec. The service has been discontinued.

Peter Pan Bus Lines of Springfield, Massachusetts, has a fleet of 132 Motor Coach Industries buses. The one pictured here is a 1997 45-foot Model 102DL3. The company, a member of the Trailways Transportation System, has a main route between Boston and Washington, D.C. via New York City and Baltimore. The graphics with the Peter Pan story theme appear on the sides of each of the Peter Pan Bus Lines buses.

This 1997 MCI 102DL3 has a Caterpillar C10 350-hp diesel engine and an Allison automatic transmission. It has the optional MCI trailer towing package so it can be used to pull the Greyhound Courier Express trailers.

A large part of Greyhound Canada's revenue comes from bus parcel express. Even the large baggage compartments of a 45-foot coach cannot carry this volume of freight, so MCI offers a trailering option for extra capacity. A fully loaded trailer can weigh 10,000 lbs.

Grey Goose of Winnipeg, Manitoba, has some high volume freight runs that need a 54-passenger Motor Coach Industries Model 102DL3 pulling a trailer. This is a 1999 DL3, fleet number 1063, which works the ten-hour schedule between Winnipeg and Thompson, Manitoba.

This MCI 102DL3 was so new to Greyhound Canada service that the dog decal had not yet been applied as it is shown pulling out of the Greyhound Winnipeg shop. Of special interest is that this coach has a trailer towing package and is wheelchair lift equipped, the combination being a first for Greyhound Canada as well as a first for MCI. This coach, fleet number 1128, was built in June 2000, and 11 more of these coaches entered service for Greyhound Canada about the same time. They are powered by the Detroit Diesel Series 60 engine and the B500 Allison automatic transmission.

Motor Coach Industries introduced the Renaissance® Coach at the American Bus Association annual meeting in Hawaii in 1996. This new model was the result of 200 "person years" of effort in the research and design phases. One of the special features of the bus is a curved entrance stairway.

Trentway-Wagar Inc. of Peterborough, Ontario, was one of the first bus companies to add the Motor Coach Industries Renaissance® Coach to its fleet. Eight were delivered in 1998 with more added in 1999. Trentway-Wagar operates the Montreal-Toronto route and also provides considerable service in Southern Ontario west of Toronto. Trentway-Wagar is a Coach Canada company.

Shown in Las Vegas in 1998, this MCI 102ELS3 conversion coach gives an idea of the space available for a custom designed interior. The 102ELS3 features a raised roof line for additional interior space. As far back as the 1950s, Motor Coach Industries has offered partially completed coaches for conversion projects. Photo Credit: *Andrew Gold photo*

Many Motor Coach Industries buses have been completed with special interiors for corporations and other businesses as well as entertainers, celebrities, and individuals. Custom Coach Corporation in Dublin, Ohio, is one of the major coach conversion companies. Pictured here is an MCI Renaissance® Coach with a special corporate interior for Dave Thomas, founder of Wendy's International. It is Thomas' 10th special coach from Custom Coach Corporation.

The 1000th Motor Coach Industries Renaissance® Coach was produced in 1999. The bus was purchased by Orion Pacific Bus Company of Brea, California, and presented to the owners of the company at *METRO* Magazine's BusCon in Las Vegas in September 1999.

Greyhound Canada fleet 1093 is shown outside the shop in Calgary. The Renaissance® Coach is proving to be a reliable coach for scheduled Greyhound service.

Specially painted for Rocky Mountaineer Railtours, this coach is from the Laidlaw charter division in Banff, Alberta. In 2000, six new Renaissance® coaches were dedicated to providing seamless service to Rocky Mountaineer Railtour guests.

Laidlaw Canadian Rockies received 12 new Renaissance® coaches for the 2000 summer season. This is fleet number 1110 posed outside the Greyhound Calgary shop.

The Motor Coach Industries F-3500 coach was introduced at BusCon in Baltimore, Maryland, September 2000. It is a two-axle, 35-foot, mid-sized coach with comfortable seating for 36 passengers. A 285-horsepower Cummins diesel engine powers the coach. The F-3500 was especially designed for small, day-tour and shuttle groups. It is also available as a conversion-ready shell to accommodate interiors as limousine/executive coaches or motorhomes.

One of the newest Motor Coach Industries coaches is referred to as the G series with two models, the G4100 and the G4500. These coaches represent a multi-million dollar research and development investment. The G4100 is a 41-foot coach and the G4500 is a 45-foot coach. Both models feature a Detroit Diesel Series 60 diesel engine, which is standard, and an Allison B-500 automatic transmission. Pictured here is the G4100. It also displays the Motor Coach Industries logo introduced in 2000.

Meet the Authors

Brian Grams

My Father drove out of Calgary for Greyhound Canada from the time I was born until his retirement. I drove for Brewster Transport and Greyhound Canada while I attended the university in Calgary.

Calgary, Alberta, is head office for Greyhound Canada and the main shop is located here, so I grew up looking at the latest and greatest offerings from MCI, many of which I drove when they later showed up in the Brewster fleet. While with Greyhound I drove brand new MCIs, which were MC-7s and MC-8s at that time. The MC-6 was still in daily use here and I would get to drive these from time to time as well.

As my interest in the coaches grew and my hobby as a photographer included taking bus photos, I was fortunate to receive many photos from others. Greyhound staff, MCI staff, and others were happy to share their photos, stories, and memories with me.

It is a true pleasure to know Bill Luke and his wife Adeline. I have written historical articles for them when they published *Bus Ride*. Bill's knowledge and background in this industry is truly phenomenal.

My working career has been spent in the bus industry and I am now responsible for disposal of used coaches from the Laidlaw group of companies. I own a number of coaches and have the oldest Canadian Greyhound known. It is a 1937 Kenworth that was new to Central Canadian Greyhound Lines. I also have one of the first MCIs, which is a 1941. Prior to 1941 MCI was called Fort Garry Motors.

I continue to gather information on the coaches built by this fine company and maintain good contact with many of the operators that continue to own MCI products.

I hope you enjoy the book and I invite questions and comments to be addressed to me at gramsb@home.com

William A. Luke

Motor Coach Industries has been familiar to me for more than 50 years. I first visited the MCI factory in 1947. That visit was followed by more friendly and enjoyable visits to see various MCI buses in production in Winnipeg and Pembina, North Dakota.

I have also traveled extensively on MCI buses. My first trip on MCI buses was in 1951 when I went to the Canadian Rockies. I rode a Western Canadian Greyhound Lines MCI Courier 100 model over many miles, often on gravel highways.

Over the years, I traveled on MCI buses operated by some 50 different bus companies in the United States and Canada. I also have traveled on MCI buses in Australia, Taiwan, Argentina and Uruguay.

On the 50th anniversary of the Alaska Highway, I rode an MCI MC-9 Greyhound bus over the Highway between Dawson Creek, British Columbia, and Whitehorse, Yukon.

As an avid bus historian and journalist, I have enjoyed writing about MCI and interviewing the many wonderful people I have met in the organization. I have found it a great leisure to travel on MCI buses and I will continue to do so.

MORE TITLES FROM ICONOGRAFIX:

All Iconografix books are available from direct mail specialty book dealers and bookstores worldwide, or can be ordered from the publisher. For book trade and distribution information or to add your name to our mailing list and receive a **FREE CATALOG** contact:

Iconografix, PO Box 446, Hudson, Wisconsin, 54016   Telephone: (715) 381-9755, (800) 289-3504 (USA), Fax: (715) 381-9756

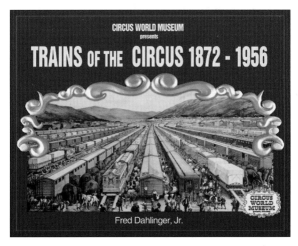
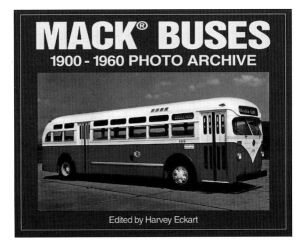
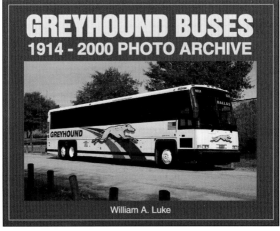
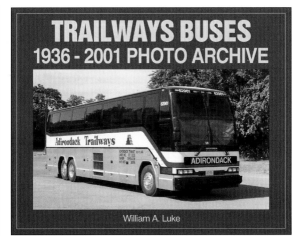